THE
NBA
A HISTORY OF HOOPS

Published by Creative Education
P.O. Box 227, Mankato, Minnesota 56002
Creative Education is an imprint of The Creative Company
www.thecreativecompany.us

Design and production by Christine Vanderbeek
Art direction by Rita Marshall

Printed by Corporate Graphics in the United States of America

Photographs by AP Images, Corbis (Bettmann), Dreamstime (Munktcu), Getty Images
(Sylvester Adams, Andrew D. Bernstein/NBAE, Nathaniel S. Butler/NBAE, Scott
Cunningham/NBAE, Jerry Driendl, Focus on Sport, Jesse D. Garrabrant/NBAE, Noah
Graham/NBAE, Walter Iooss Jr./NBAE, Walter Iooss Jr./Sports Illustrated, Ken Levine/
Allsport, George Long/WireImage, Richard Meek/Sports Illustrated, Rogers Photo Archive,
Bob Rosato/Sports Illustrated, SM/AIUEO, Kent Smith/NBAE, Damian Strohmeyer/Sports
Illustrated), iStockphoto (Brandon Laufenberg), US Presswire (Malcolm Emmons)

Library of Congress Cataloging-in-Publication Data
Omoth, Tyler.
The story of the Atlanta Hawks / by Tyler Omoth.
p. cm. — (The NBA: a history of hoops)
Includes index.
Summary: The history of the Atlanta Hawks professional basketball
team from its start as the Tri-Cities Blackhawks in 1946 to today,
spotlighting the franchise's greatest players and moments.
ISBN 978-1-58341-936-6
1. Atlanta Hawks (Basketball team)—History—Juvenile literature.
I. Title. II. Series.
GV885.52.A7O6 2010   796.323'6409758231—dc22   2009034775

CPSIA: 120109 PO1093

First Edition
2 4 6 8 9 7 5 3 1

Page 3: Point guard Mike Bibby
Pages 4–5: Forward Josh Smith

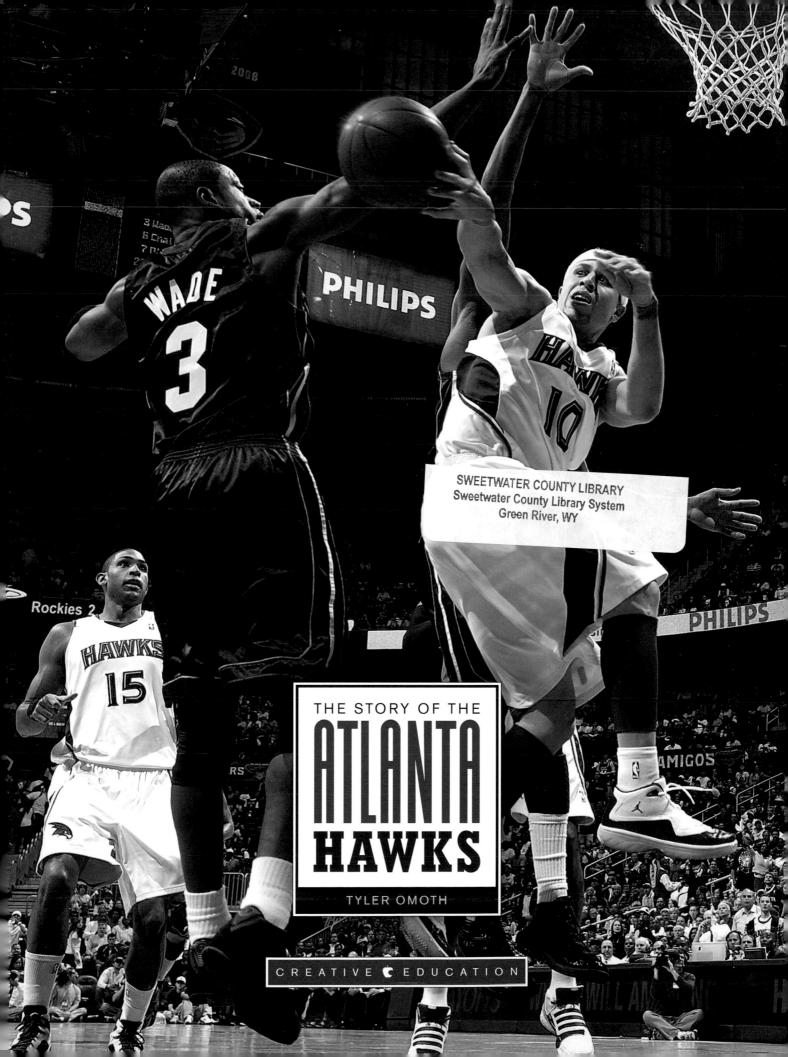

THE STORY OF THE

ATLANTA HAWKS

TYLER OMOTH

CREATIVE ● EDUCATION

CONTENTS

CHAPTER ONE

THE HAWKS TAKE FLIGHT

Compared with older cities in the southeastern United States, early Atlanta, Georgia, seemed to be just another rough-and-tumble railway town. Its location at the southern tip of the Appalachian Mountains on the Western and Atlantic Railroad made it a center of commerce, and during the Civil War, Atlanta became one of the main supply hubs of the Confederate Army. Because of its importance, Union general William Sherman burned every building in the city that could be of use to the Confederacy as part of his infamous "March to the Sea" in 1864. After the war, Atlanta was rebuilt bigger and better.

Sports have long been an important facet of the city known as the "Crown Jewel of the South." The Atlanta Braves have been a fixture in Major League Baseball since 1966, and the

Professional sports venues—including baseball stadiums such as Turner Field (pictured, bottom)—are a key part of the Atlanta cityscape.

National Football League's Atlanta Falcons have been thrilling their fans for just as long. The National Basketball Association (NBA) arrived just after those franchises, in 1968. That was when the St. Louis Hawks, a team that had begun in the Midwest as the Tri-Cities Blackhawks, moved to town and showed local sports fans that Atlanta could compete on the basketball court as well as the diamond or gridiron.

I n 1949, two professional basketball leagues, the National Basketball League (NBL) and the Basketball Association of America (BAA), merged to become the NBA. The Tri-Cities Blackhawks were among the original 17 teams in the newly formed league. The franchise—which was shared by the neighboring cities of Rock Island, Illinois; Moline, Illinois; and Davenport, Iowa—was named in reference to the Black Hawk War that took place in the area in 1832. After the Blackhawks started 1–6 during their inaugural 1949–50 season, young coach Arnold "Red" Auerbach was hired to replace the club's original head coach, Roger Potter. Auerbach oversaw a turnaround that ended with a 29–35 record and a playoff berth. The Blackhawks lost to the Anderson Packers in the first round, and Auerbach then moved on to Boston, where he would become a coaching legend with the Celtics.

Despite the leadership and scoring of forward Dike Eddleman, the Hawks had a dismal 25–43 showing in the 1950–51 season. With fan support for the Blackhawks waning, team owner Ben Kerner moved the franchise from the Tri-Cities to Milwaukee, Wisconsin. The club, now called the Hawks, finished in the cellar of the Western Division in each of its first three seasons in Milwaukee.

Toward the end of the 1953–54 season, the Hawks made a bench change by hiring William "Red" Holzman as their new head coach. On the court, the Hawks found the star they had been lacking by selecting 6-foot-9 and 205-pound forward/center Bob Pettit in the 1954 NBA Draft. Pettit earned NBA Rookie of the Year honors by averaging 20.4 points and 13.8 rebounds per game. The young star's brilliant play couldn't lift the Hawks from the bottom of their division, though, and they finished in last place again with a 26–46 record.

After four consecutive last-place finishes in Wisconsin, Kerner announced that he was moving the team again, this time south to St. Louis, Missouri, where the Hawks were warmly welcomed. Midway through the 1955–56 season, Kerner brought in some help for Pettit and center Chuck Share by adding versatile forward Jack Coleman and steady-scoring guard Jack McMahon. The moves paid off, as St. Louis made it into the playoffs in both 1956 and 1957. In 1957, the Hawks swept the Minneapolis Lakers in the opening round of the postseason to reach the NBA Finals, where they faced the heavily favored Celtics. Led by Pettit and forward Cliff Hagan, the Hawks put up a good fight but came up just short, four games to three.

INTRODUCING...

BOB PETTIT

POSITION FORWARD / CENTER
HEIGHT 6-FOOT-9
HAWKS SEASONS 1954–65

BASKETBALL WASN'T NECESSARILY EASY FOR BOB PETTIT. He was cut from his Baton Rouge, Louisiana, high school basketball team as a freshman and then again as a sophomore. His father encouraged him to push himself by working on shooting and footwork fundamentals tirelessly at home. Putting in more effort than the next player became Pettit's trademark in high school, college, and all the way through an 11-season NBA career. When he entered the league in 1954, people still doubted his ability to match up against more physically gifted athletes. Yet Pettit was an All-Star in every season of his career and retired as the very first player in the NBA to reach 20,000 career points. For more than a decade, he was the centerpiece of the Hawks franchise, never finishing lower than fifth in the league in rebounding or fourth in scoring. "Bob made 'second effort' a part of the sport's vocabulary," said Hall of Fame Celtics center Bill Russell. "He kept coming at you more than any man in the game. He was always battling for position, fighting you off the boards."

WHEN A PLAYER IS TRADED BEFORE HE PLAYS A SINGLE NBA GAME, EVEN WHEN IT'S FOR ANOTHER GREAT PLAYER, HE OFTEN BECOMES EVEN MORE DETERMINED TO PROVE HIS WORTH. Cliff Hagan did just that for the Hawks for 10 seasons. After being picked in the third round of the 1953 NBA Draft by the Celtics, he was traded to the St. Louis Hawks (along with forward Ed Macauley) for center Bill Russell. Fans called Hagan "Li'l Abner" because of his innocent looks, but there was nothing innocent about how he played. Hagan was a pure shooter who could put points on the board at a furious pace, and he instantly made the Hawks a much stronger team with his smooth and accurate hook shot. Everywhere he went, Hagan helped build championships. He won the national college championship with the University of Kentucky Wildcats in 1951, the NBA championship in 1958 with the Hawks, and when he spent two years in the military in 1954 and 1955, he was a part of the Worldwide Air Force championship team both years.

AFTER LOSING THE NBA FINALS TO THE CELTICS IN A DOUBLE-OVERTIME GAME 7 IN 1957, THE ST. LOUIS HAWKS WELCOMED A REMATCH AGAINST THEIR NEMESIS IN THE SPRING OF 1958. No one wanted to beat the Celtics more than forward Bob Pettit, who had missed a last-second shot attempt to lose the heartbreaking series in 1957. After two games, the 1958 Finals series was tied at one win apiece. During Game 3, star Celtics center Bill Russell sprained his ankle and was forced to take a seat on the bench. St. Louis won two of the next three contests. When the series came back to St. Louis for Game 6, Russell returned for the Celtics, but Pettit was determined to win it all. By halftime, he had tallied 19 points to stake the Hawks to a 57–52 lead. After the Celtics surged back to capture a two-point lead in the fourth quarter, Pettit took charge. The star forward scored 19 of the Hawks' final 21 points (and a total of 50 for the game) to bring the championship to St. Louis.

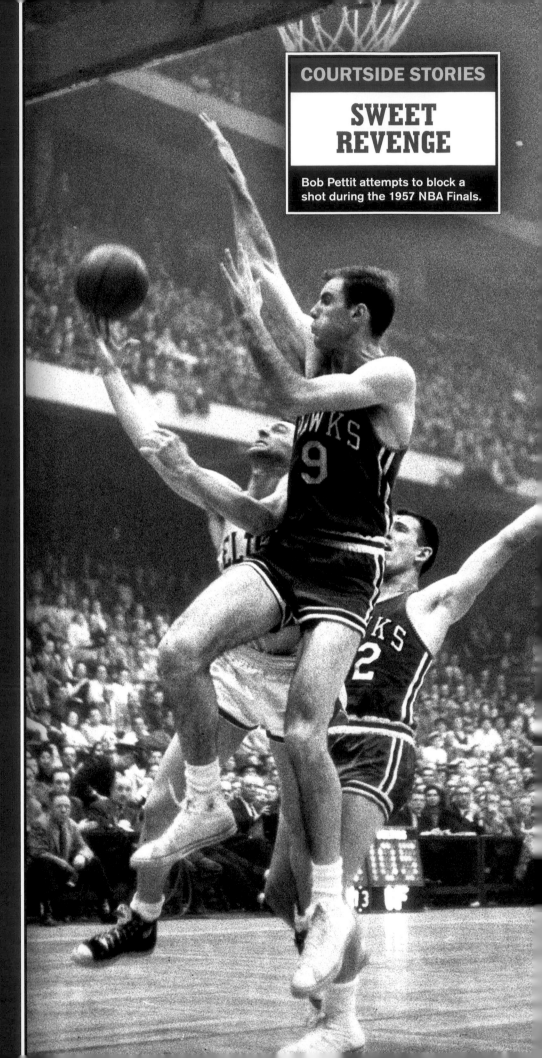

COURTSIDE STORIES

SWEET REVENGE

Bob Pettit attempts to block a shot during the 1957 NBA Finals.

One year wiser and more experienced, the Hawks charged to the top of the Western Division standings and stayed there throughout the 1957–58 season. St. Louis topped the Detroit Pistons in the first round of the playoffs and once again met the Celtics in the Finals. This time, the Hawks would not be denied, winning the NBA title four games to two. Pettit, who was sensational in the series, soaked up the experience, later saying, "It was a great feeling. It was the highlight of my 11-year professional career, no doubt. It's something you look back on forever."

With Cliff Hagan in uniform, the Hawks were a perennial contender, making the playoffs in 9 of the 10 seasons from 1956–57 to 1965–66.

CHAPTER TWO

ON TO ATLANTA

The Hawks remained a contender through the early 1960s. New stars such as crafty point guard Lenny Wilkens and bruising center Clyde Lovellette were added to the lineup, but the team never quite regained the championship magic of 1958. Still led by Pettit and Hagan, the Hawks returned to the NBA Finals in 1961 but were defeated by the Celtics, four games to one. The next season, Wilkens was called to active military duty, sending the Hawks to a dismal 29–51 record. The next few seasons ended with winning records but early playoff exits, and in 1965, Pettit retired. Then, after the Hawks assembled another winning season in 1967–68, Kerner shocked St. Louis by announcing his decision to sell the team to a group of Atlanta businessmen who intended to relocate the team. St. Louis had seen the last of the Hawks.

Before taking the court for the first time in Atlanta, the team parted ways with Wilkens by trading him to the Seattle Super-Sonics for guard Walt Hazzard. With Hazzard in the backcourt and Zelmo Beaty, a prolific scorer, at center, the Hawks were ready to fly for their new fans. The move to Atlanta was made

Known as "Jumping Joe" or "Pogo Joe" on account of his terrific leaping ability, forward Joe Caldwell netted 21.1 points a game in 1969–70.

even smoother by third-year swingman Lou Hudson's emergence as a star. After finishing the season 48–34, the Hawks defeated the San Diego Rockets to advance to the Western Division finals. Unfortunately, the Los Angeles Lakers were too powerful, stopping the Hawks in five games.

The 1969–70 season was strikingly similar. Hudson finished fifth in the league in scoring, averaging 25.4 points per game, while guiding the Hawks to another 48–34 record. Atlanta eliminated the Chicago Bulls from the playoffs on its way to the division finals, where it again met Los Angeles. This time, star guard Jerry West and dominant center Wilt Chamberlain proved to be even better than before, and the Lakers swept the Hawks in four straight games.

The NBA was realigned in 1970, and the 1970–71 Hawks found themselves in the Central Division of the new Eastern Conference. Before the season began, the team lost its second-best scorer from the previous year, forward "Pogo Joe" Caldwell, as he jumped from the NBA to the rival American Basketball Association (ABA). It was a problem that was a constant source of frustration for the Hawks and their fans. "We'd

Before joining the NBA in 1970, Pete Maravich had become an amateur legend by averaging 44.2 points per game throughout his college career.

just get a good bunch together, and then we'd lose one or two of them," complained Hawks coach Richie Guerin after the ABA lured away Beaty and Caldwell in successive seasons.

The team partially made up for the loss of those standouts by drafting flashy point guard "Pistol" Pete Maravich, college basketball's all-time scoring leader, in 1970. The rookie was an immediate fan favorite, entertaining the crowds in Atlanta's Alexander Memorial Coliseum with his no-look passes and extraordinary ball-handling. But despite the best efforts of the mop-haired Maravich, the Hawks were quickly bounced from the playoffs in each of his first two years. After the Celtics eliminated the Hawks in the first round of the 1973 playoffs, Atlanta's postseason run was over, and four straight losing seasons would follow. In 1974, Maravich was traded to the New Orleans Jazz, leaving fans with little to cheer about except Hudson's scoring exploits. "Sweet Lou" would lead the charge until 1977, when he was traded to the Lakers.

Meanwhile, the ABA dealt the Hawks another blow in 1975. Hoping to begin rebuilding a winner, Atlanta drafted highflying swingman David Thompson and shot-blocking center Marvin Webster with the first and third picks of the NBA Draft. Both players, however, opted to sign with the ABA's Denver Nuggets instead of the Hawks, and Atlanta finished at the bottom of its division.

NO TEAM IN THE NBA HAS EMBRACED A FAST, EXCITING STYLE OF BASKETBALL SYMBOLIZED BY THE SLAM DUNK QUITE LIKE THE ATLANTA HAWKS. And in the 1970s, no player represented the dunk better than swingman Julius "Dr. J" Erving. "No one has ever controlled and conquered the air above pro basketball like Julius Erving," noted sportswriter Pete Axthelm. For a very brief period before the 1972–73 season, the Hawks had the ultimate highflier. After playing his rookie pro season with the ABA's Virginia Squires, Erving decided that he could make more money in the NBA and signed a $2-million contract with Atlanta. Eventually, a grievance lodged by the Squires won out, and Erving was ordered to honor his original contract. However, for three exhibition games (two of them Atlanta wins), Erving wore Hawks red and white alongside guard "Pistol" Pete Maravich. "The most memorable part of it was the raw talent on the court," said *The Atlanta Journal-Constitution* writer Mike McKenzie. "Everyone just stopped what they were doing to watch Maravich and Erving do their shtick. Together, they were unstoppable."

The subpar seasons of the mid-1970s were hard on the Atlanta franchise, which began losing fan support and revenue, and it was widely rumored that the Hawks would be forced to relocate yet again. All talk of another move was put to rest in January 1977, however, when Ted Turner, a wealthy media mogul, bought the Hawks and stabilized their position in Atlanta.

With the Hawks' financial problems behind them, the team's fortunes began to rise. In the 1977 NBA Draft, Atlanta chose 7-foot-1 and 250-pound center Wayne "Tree" Rollins, who gave the team a fearsome defensive presence under the basket. "Tree is the type of guy you hope to have around for 10 years," noted Hawks coach Hubie Brown. "He has a great work ethic and gives you everything he has every night."

The 1977–78 Hawks posted an improved 41–41 record and made a return to the playoffs but were quickly sent home by the Washington Bullets. As the 1980s began, Rollins, guard Charlie Criss, and forward Dan Roundfield formed the core of some solid Atlanta teams. But the Hawks knew they still needed to add a top-tier scoring threat if they were going to challenge the NBA's elite.

LOU HUDSON

POSITION FORWARD / GUARD
HEIGHT 6-FOOT-5
HAWKS SEASONS 1966–77

WHEN ST. LOUIS HAWKS SCOUTS SAW A SENIOR SWINGMAN AT THE UNIVERSITY OF MINNESOTA TALLY 30 POINTS IN A 1966 GAME DESPITE HAVING A BROKEN HAND, THEY KNEW THAT THEY WERE WATCHING A SPECIAL PLAYER.

In the next NBA Draft, the Hawks took "Sweet" Lou Hudson with the fourth overall selection. Although every part of Hudson's game was fluid, he was best known for having one of the smoothest jump shots in basketball. His scoring ability and consistent effort made him an invaluable member of the Hawks for 11 seasons and a 6-time All-Star. In a 1967 game against the Bulls, Hudson put up 57 points, a total that still stands as the highest single-game total in club history. He averaged 20.2 points per game over his career and, as of 2010, was 1 of only 3 Hawks players to have his jersey number (23) retired. Cotton Fitzsimmons, who coached Hudson with the Hawks in the early 1970s, loved to watch Sweet Lou shoot the ball. "Even though players can shoot today," he said in 2003, "I haven't seen anyone shoot any better."

CHAPTER THREE

THE DOMINIQUE YEARS

On September 2, 1982, the Hawks made a trade with the Utah Jazz for the draft rights to University of Georgia standout Dominique Wilkins, giving them the offensive star they had been lacking. In his rookie year, the 6-foot-7 and 215-pound forward averaged 17.5 points a game. Yet despite the young star's heroics, the team still could not make a deep push into the playoffs. Atlanta fell to the Celtics and the hot shooting of forward Larry Bird in the first round, losing two games to one. After two seasons of disappointing postseason performances, a new coach, Mike Fratello, was hired to try his hand at turning the Hawks around.

Tree Rollins was an elite shot blocker, capable of thwarting even such superstars as Chicago Bulls guard Michael Jordan (pictured).

MIKE FRATELLO WAS A LITTLE MAN IN A BIG MAN'S GAME. When the struggling Hawks were looking for a new direction in 1983, they handed the clipboard to Fratello, a passionate fighter with big ideas. In high school, the tenacious, 5-foot-7 and 150-pound Fratello had earned a football scholarship to New Jersey's Montclair State University as a center and nose tackle. After having made quick playoff exits for two straight seasons, Atlanta needed a leader with that kind of fierce, resilient attitude. Fratello's strengths were his deep knowledge of the game and his knack for strategy. In the mid-1980s, he led the Hawks to 4 consecutive seasons of at least 50 wins, including a 57–25 season (1986–87) that still stands as the best in club history. After his coaching days, Fratello became a basketball analyst for the TNT television studio, and his affinity for diagramming plays on-screen earned him the nickname "The Czar of the Telestrator." Star Hawks forward Dominique Wilkins appreciated Fratello's hard-nosed style, saying, "A lot of times you hated him, but he knew how to win."

INTRODUCING...

MIKE FRATELLO

COACH
HAWKS SEASONS 1980, 1983–90

To support Wilkins, Fratello and the Hawks added impressive performers such as guards Anthony "Spud" Webb and Glenn "Doc" Rivers and muscular forward Kevin Willis. In 1986–87, this new Atlanta lineup posted a franchise-best 57–25 record. Leading the way was Wilkins, who finished second in the league in scoring with 29 points a game. In the playoffs, the Hawks fought past the Indiana Pacers in the first round to earn a showdown with the Pistons and their star point guard, Isiah Thomas. The two Eastern Conference powers slugged it out for five games, but the Hawks came up short.

When he entered the NBA in 1985 as a member of the Hawks, 5-foot-7 point guard Spud Webb was the shortest player in league history.

HAWKS ARE HIGHFLYING AND POTENTIALLY DAN-GEROUS CREATURES. In Atlanta, no Hawks player fit that description better than Dominique Wilkins. Known league-wide as "The Human Highlight Film," Wilkins was one of the most spectacular slam-dunk artists in NBA history. To the Hawks, though, he was more than just a dunk specialist; he was their primary scoring machine.

Long and slim, Wilkins played the game with amazing speed and agility. He could bury long-range jumpers, played excellent defense, and had the leaping ability to soar over virtually any defender. When he reached the rim, it was often with a thunderous windmill slam that would bring Atlanta fans to their feet. Former Hawks guard Mike Glenn recalled watching Wilkins score 23

points in his NBA rookie debut, saying, "That night, we saw the raw energy and passion that Dominique brought to the game, and we saw the kind of work ethic that would lead him to become one of the best scorers the game has ever seen." Wilkins retired from basketball in 1999 with 26,668 career points. As of 2010, only nine other players in NBA history had scored more.

The next season was a virtual replay. Coach Fratello guided the Hawks to a 50–32 mark, and again his team fought into the second round of the playoffs. This time Atlanta's opponent was Boston. Fans were treated to a thrilling show as Wilkins and Boston star Larry Bird staged a classic shootout, but in the end, the Celtics triumphed. After adding imposing center Moses Malone to help work the boards, Atlanta improved to 52–30 in 1988–89, but it made a quick exit from the playoffs. The Hawks then took a step backward as they concluded the 1980s with an injury-plagued season that ended 41–41 and left them out of the postseason.

Wilkins, who was nicknamed "The Human Highlight Film" on account of his acrobatic slam dunks and spectacular athleticism, continued to thrill Atlanta fans through the 1993–94 season, when the Hawks decided to rebuild. In February 1994, Atlanta made the controversial decision to trade Wilkins to the Los Angeles Clippers. "That trade ruined pro basketball in Atlanta," noted *Sports Illustrated* writer Lang Whitaker. "You can make bad trades, you can make trades that set a franchise back a few years, or you can make moves that completely ruin a sport in a city. Atlanta lost their only NBA hero, and from then on things plummeted downhill."

The Hawks were indeed weakened by Wilkins's departure in the mid-1990s, despite the additions of such players as guards Steve Smith and Mookie Blaylock. Even the leadership of Lenny Wilkens, who had returned to the team in 1993 as its head coach, could not earn Atlanta much playoff success. A central problem was that the Hawks' lack of a talented big man left them vulnerable to inside attacks. "Championship teams start from the inside out," noted Coach Wilkens. "We need a stronger presence down low in order to contend."

Wilkens got his wish in 1996 when the Hawks signed center Dikembe Mutombo. The 7-foot-2 Mutombo had already established himself as one of the game's most daunting shot blockers and rebounders. In his first 5 NBA seasons with the Denver Nuggets, he had averaged 12.9 points, 12.3 rebounds, and 3.8 blocked shots a game. "He's an intimidator," said forward Alan Henderson, another new addition to the Atlanta lineup. "Now he's our intimidator."

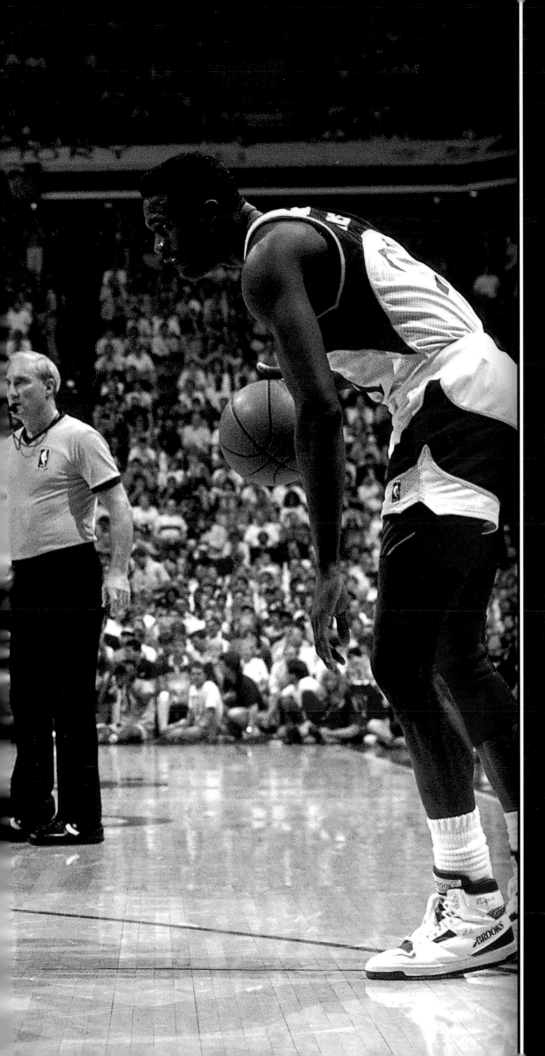

THE SECOND-ROUND MATCHUP
BETWEEN THE ATLANTA HAWKS
AND BOSTON CELTICS IN THE 1988
EASTERN CONFERENCE PLAYOFFS
WAS A CLASSIC BATTLE OF BAS-
KETBALL STYLE. The Hawks were a
thrill ride of a team, with soaring dunks
and fast action, while the Celtics were
a fundamentally strong team featuring
rugged play under the rim. Both had
a knack for winning. The Celtics won
the first two games before the Hawks
claimed the next three. When Boston
won Game 6, the stage was set for
a Game 7 clash, and the teams' two
top stars, forwards Dominique Wilkins
and Larry Bird, were ready. Wilkins
netted 16 points in the fourth quarter
by way of difficult jumpers and highflying drives to the hoop. Bird, however,
had an answer and then some, putting
up 20 points in the final quarter with
spot-up shooting and hustle. Although
the Celtics came out on top, 118–116,
everyone knew they'd seen one of the
all-time great sports duels. "It was like
watching two great gunfighters," said
Celtics forward Kevin McHale, "wait-
ing for one of them to blink. It was
unbelievable."

WHEN A TEAM IS LACKING DIREC-
TION, WHO BETTER TO TURN TO
THAN A SAILOR? Ted Turner was
one of America's most notable self-
made men, and his name is practically
synonymous with Atlanta today. At one
point, Turner's companies owned the
Hawks, Major League Baseball's
Atlanta Braves, and the National
Hockey League's Atlanta Thrashers.
Turner Communications Group pur-
chased the Hawks in 1977 when the
city was in danger of losing its NBA
franchise. At the time, the Hawks were
floundering after four consecutive losing seasons. Turner, on the other hand,
had just won the America's Cup at the
helm of his racing yacht *Courageous*.
During the Hawks' 24 years under
Turner's ownership, the team made the
playoffs 18 times. In 2004, the Hawks
raised a banner and retired the number
17—in honor of Turner's first media pur-
chase, Channel 17—while playing the
Frank Sinatra ballad "My Way" over the
public address system. "He is one of
the most colorful owners we've ever
had," said NBA commissioner David
Stern. "No one has been as loyal and
as committed as he was."

INTRODUCING...

TED TURNER

TEAM OWNER
HAWKS SEASONS 1977–2001

"**M**ount Mutombo" instantly improved the Hawks. Still, three straight records of 56–26, 50–32, and 31–19 (during a 1998–99 season shortened by a labor dispute between NBA players and owners) were followed by three early exits in the playoffs. The Hawks were again tough defensively, but they now lacked offensive punch. In 1999, both Smith and Blaylock left the team.

Even so, the Hawks had reasons to be excited as the 1999–2000 season began. For one, they were moving into their new, state-of-the-art home, Philips Arena. For another, Atlanta had just selected speedy guard Jason Terry with the 10th overall pick of the 1999 NBA Draft. But even though Terry had a solid rookie season, and Mutombo won the NBA rebounding title with 14.1 boards per game, the Hawks still finished a mere 28–54.

SOME BIRDS ARE KNOWN FOR MIGRATING, AND THE ATLANTA HAWKS ARE AMONG THEM. Over the years, the Hawks have called eight different arenas home, which is more than almost any other NBA team. The Hawks were born as the Tri-Cities Blackhawks and played their first games in the Wharton Field House in Moline, Illinois. Then it was on to Milwaukee and the Milwaukee Arena. When the team flew south to St. Louis, it spent time at the Kiel Auditorium and in the St. Louis Arena. In Atlanta, the franchise landed in the Alexander Memorial Coliseum. After a long stint in the Omni Coliseum, a return to the Alexander, and then two years at the Georgia Dome, the Hawks finally found a comfortable home in 1999. Philips Arena, built to accommodate the Hawks and the Atlanta Thrashers hockey team, featured a unique design that used exterior columns to spell out "Atlanta" and "CNN," making it a visual tribute to its hometown and sponsor. "We were looking to design a building that was timeless," said Bernardo Fort Brescia, a member of the arena's design team.

CHAPTER FOUR

THE HAWKS RISE AGAIN

For the next five seasons, the story of the Hawks was one of frustrated hopes. The 2000–01 season marked a new low as Atlanta finished 25–57. The next season saw key additions such as shot-blocking center Theo Ratliff and forward Shareef Abdur-Rahim suit up alongside Terry, who had become a legitimate star. Still, from 2000–01 to 2004–05, the team managed only a combined 134–276 record. The 2004–05 season was the worst yet, as Atlanta finished at the bottom of the NBA with an embarrassing 13–69 mark.

Despite that season's terrible record, the Hawks had built a foundation for the future by obtaining athletic guard Josh Childress and electrifying forward Josh Smith in the 2004 NBA Draft. Both rookies improved as the 2004–05 season progressed, newly acquired forward Al Harrington boosted the offense with 17.5 points per game, and new coach Mike Woodson began instilling an unselfish, "team-first" attitude in his young players.

Josh Childress (right) contributed to Atlanta's rebounding effort from day one, snaring six boards a game as a rookie in 2004–05.

The Hawks accrued more talent in the 2005 NBA Draft by picking up two promising rookies: Marvin Williams, an explosive, 6-foot-9 forward, and Salim Stoudamire, a guard with a knack for hitting clutch shots. Although inexperienced, the Hawks lineup was eager to make its mark. "I want to win," Williams said. "We're all going to work hard. We're going to be young, but at least we're going to learn the game of basketball from the coaches."

The Hawks' abundance of young athleticism, as well as the addition of experienced guard Joe Johnson, gave Atlanta fans hope heading into 2005–06. Johnson quickly won over the home crowd, leading the club in points, assists, and three-pointers as the team fought to a 26–56 record, doubling its victory total from the previous season. With a roster of players averaging just 23 years of age, the Hawks looked like a team that was finally ready to fly.

Unfortunately, the story of 2006–07 was injuries. Atlanta had only six games all season long in which all seven of its best players were healthy at the same time, making it difficult to have any consistency on the court. With Johnson scoring 25 points per game and Smith developing into a star on both ends of the court, the Hawks battled through their ailments to improve once again to 30–52.

A superb scorer, passer, and defender, guard Joe Johnson earned invitations to the NBA All-Star Game in 2007, 2008, 2009, and 2010.

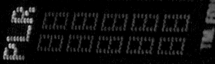

IT'S ONLY FITTING THAT A TEAM NAMED THE HAWKS WOULD HAVE PLAYERS WHO CAN FLY.

In 1984, the NBA made the Slam Dunk Contest a regular part of the All-Star Game weekend, giving some of the most athletic players in the league a chance to showcase their best dunks. Not surprisingly, it was "The Human Highlight Film," Dominique Wilkins, who first brought home the Slam Dunk trophy for the Hawks. He topped another legendary dunker, Chicago Bulls guard Michael Jordan, in the 1985 contest with an off-the-backboard reverse slam and a thrilling wind-mill dunk. The next year, 5-foot-7 Hawks guard Spud Webb wowed NBA fans and even amazed his peers with his aerial acrobatics to beat out Wilkins for the title. In 1990, Wilkins brought home his second trophy.

A decade and a half later, forward Josh Smith wore a number 21 jersey to honor Wilkins when he unveiled his own windmill slam en route to winning the 2005 contest. By 2010, the Atlanta highfliers' four Slam Dunk crowns totaled more than any other team in the NBA to date.

I n 2007–08, Johnson earned a spot in the NBA All-Star Game for the second season in a row, and rookie center Al Horford—the third overall pick in the 2007 NBA Draft—became an immediate triple threat as a scorer, rebounder, and shot blocker. Improved defense and a high-energy style of play boosted Atlanta to 37–45, good enough to claim the eighth and final spot in the Eastern Conference playoffs. For the first time since 1999, Atlanta was in the postseason.

The Hawks' first-round opponent was the 66–16 Celtics, creating a David-versus-Goliath matchup in which Atlanta was an obvious under-dog. Yet after the Celtics handled the young Atlanta team easily in the first two games, the Hawks rebounded to win the next two. After splitting the next two games, the two teams had the eyes of the sports world upon them as they traveled back to Boston for a deciding Game 7. The veteran Celtics (who would go on to win the NBA championship) won 99–65 to claim the game and the series, but the Hawks came away with a new level of respect league-wide.

The fast-improving Hawks opened the next season with six straight victories. Newly acquired guard Ronald "Flip" Murray added versatility and extra scoring off the bench, while Horford, Smith, and Willams continued to mature. After witnessing firsthand during the previous season's playoff series with the Celtics how a smothering defense can control and

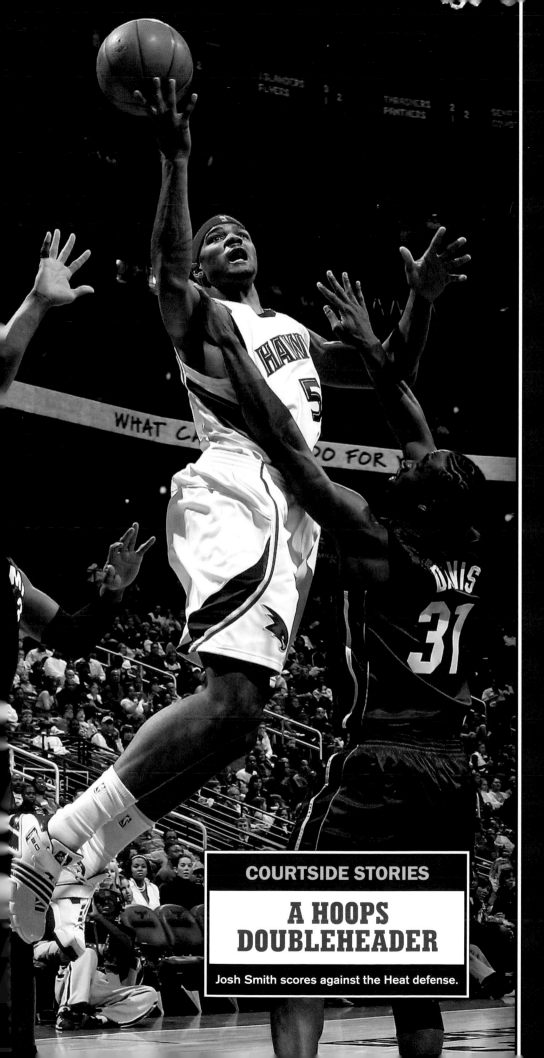

COURTSIDE STORIES

A HOOPS DOUBLEHEADER

Josh Smith scores against the Heat defense.

THE DOUBLEHEADER, OR BACK-TO-BACK GAMES IN ONE DAY, IS USUALLY A BASEBALL THING, BUT IN MARCH 2008, THE HAWKS PUT TWO WINS ON THEIR RECORD AGAINST THE MIAMI HEAT, THANKS TO A VERY RARE "DO-OVER" MANDATED BY THE LEAGUE—THE FIRST SUCH DO-OVER SINCE 1983. The game tipped off on December 19, 2007, but when Heat center Shaquille O'Neal committed his fifth foul late in overtime, the official scorer mistakenly indicated that he had fouled out. The Hawks won 117–111, but when the mistake was brought to light, the league ordered the two teams to play out the time that had elapsed after the mistake. (O'Neal, however, didn't play because the Heat had traded him to the Phoenix Suns in early February.) The two teams played out the 51.9 seconds without any further scoring, and Atlanta officially won the game again, 114–111. "We made every play we needed to make in those 51 seconds," said Hawks coach Mike Woodson. The Hawks doused the Heat in the second game as well, helping Atlanta make the playoffs for the first time since 1999.

win games, the Hawks tuned in to what Coach Woodson had been preaching, earning a 47–35 mark by season's end. "Our defense is the one constant, the one thing we've been able to count on every night so far," said Woodson. "It's not always the prettiest thing to the casual eye, but it's what wins in our league."

After topping the Miami Heat in seven games to win their first playoff series in a decade, the Hawks were swept by the Cleveland Cavaliers and superstar forward LeBron James in round two. Atlanta kept the momentum going in 2009–10, though, surging to 53–29, then winning another playoff series, this time over the Milwaukee Bucks. "It's been a good season," said Horford, who emerged as one of the NBA's top rebounders. "But there's more to the team than just this."

Since they first grew wings in the Tri-Cities in 1949, the Hawks have earned a reputation as one of the NBA's most exciting and colorful teams. The franchise boasts an all-time roster of stars ranging from the relentless Bob Pettit to the rim-rocking Dominique Wilkins, and it has experienced seasons at the very top of the league and at the very bottom. Now, as they enter the franchise's seventh decade of play, today's Hawks are dreaming of the highest of flights once again.

Atlanta fans counted on the continued improvement of young forward Marvin Williams to boost the Hawks higher in 2010–11 and beyond.

INDEX